Old Midmar and Cromar
including Torphins and Lumphanan
by
David Jamieson and W. Stewart Wilson

The shop in Comers, Midmar, was situated on the gable end of the property next to House of Comers. The shop was opened in October 1877 and as well as selling groceries the sign above the shop indicated that it was also a dispensing chemist (James Milne was the chemist) and the post office. The shop continued to serve the community until 2001 when the then owners retired. Together with the adjacent house it was advertised as a going concern or with development opportunities. Full planning permission had already being granted and thus the detached dwelling house was sold and the adjoining shop, steading, and stores were converted for use as a house.

Text © David Jamieson and W. Stewart Wilson, 2006.
First Published in the United Kingdom, 2006
Stenlake Publishing Limited
54–58 Mill Square
Catrine
KA5 6RD
www.stenlake.co.uk

ISBN 9781840333787

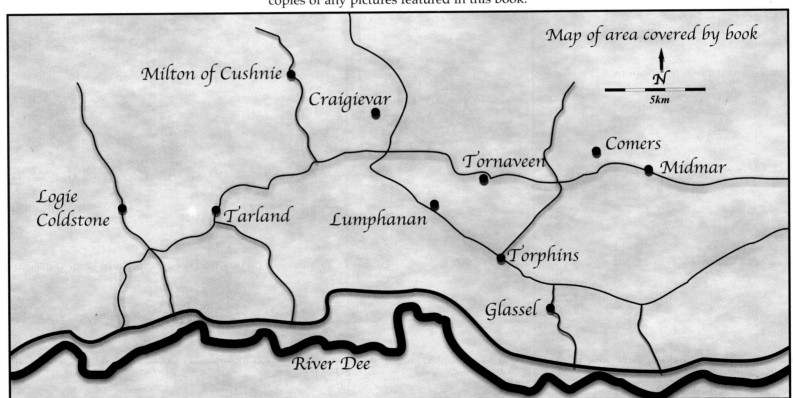

Map of area covered by book

N

5km

Milton of Cushnie

Craigievar

Comers

Midmar

Tornaveen

Logie
Coldstone

Tarland

Lumphanan

Torphins

Glassel

River Dee

INTRODUCTION

The districts of Aberdeenshire covered in this book lie 'twixt Dee and Don'. This description gives a geographical location but suggests that only these two great rivers are worthy of note. However the moors, valleys and villages which are described in this book have been hosts to many important events in the history, not only of the North East but of Scotland as a whole. There is clear evidence of past history to be seen in the stone circles, fortifications and battle sites and in the naming of dwellings and villages.

The two collective names for this area are Cromar and Midmar. Traditionally these are two of the three great divisions of the Province of Mar, the third being Braemar. It is believed that in Pictish times Mar formed one of the seven provinces of what is now called Scotland. The origin of the name Mar, or Marr, is not known but it is suggested that it may be derived from a tribal name, Vacomagi, given by the Romans to the local inhabitants.

Cromar (Cro-mharr), possibly meaning the 'circle of Mar' in Gaelic, is sometimes compared to an imprint crater, with Tarland at its centre, surrounded by a circle of hills. Some scholars prefer an alternative derivation - the 'sheepfold of Mar' (Crodh-marr). The parishes which make up Cromar are primarily Coull, Tarland and Migvie, and Logie-Coldstone (originally Logie-Mar and Coldstone). To the east of Cromar lies Midmar which derives its name either from its position as midway between the Dee and the Don or from the earlier form of the name Migmar, which appears in the older records, and has the meaning 'bog of Mar' in Gaelic.

A magnificent stone circle dating from the third century BC can be seen at Tomnaverie, on a hilltop south of Tarland, and in the parish of Midmar the early history of the area is evident in various stone circles, with a particularly good example at Sunhoney. In his writings, published in the 1940s, Dr W. Douglas Simpson traces the archaeological evidence for the occupation of the area from Neolithic times to the eighteenth century and provides a clear and authoritative outline of the importance of Mar to the development of Scotland.

The first historical event in the Province for which we have documentary evidence is a description of the pursuit and killing of Macbeth near Lumphanan in August 1057. This has been described as the period when 'Mar formed the theatre of war in this decisive struggle so pregnant with results for the future development of Scotland'. During the twelfth and thirteenth centuries the control of Mar moved from the Celtic province into a feudal earldom and the lands were ruled by a few families among which the Durwards were prominent. Their name came from being the hereditary Door Wards of the Kings of Scotland and their early fortress was at the Peel Ring at Lumphanan. Later they built Coull Castle and from there they ruled over their Barony of Onele or Oniel, a name preserved in Kincardine O'Neil. However, the raids of King Edward I into the area in 1296 and the subsequent wars proved the downfall (literally) of several of the fortifications including Coull. In the following two centuries several new families such as the Forbes, Gordons and Farquharsons came into prominence. Their refurbishment of old fortresses and the construction of fortified houses in the mid-sixteenth century are evident throughout Mar and this development 'reached its most sublime' in the building of Craigievar in 1626 by the Forbes family.

The *Statistical Account of Scotland*, written in the late eighteenth century, gives a detailed account of life in the parishes. However, the *New Statistical Account* of the 1840s shows the improvement that had been made throughout the intervening years in agriculture, communications and village life. A turnpike road had been built to connect Tarland and Aberdeen and in 1842 the description of Tarland reads: 'In the village there is a commodious and well frequented inn; five ale houses; a daily post and stamp-office; 8 shops containing grocery, and all articles generally required for domestic and agricultural purposes.' For the parish of Midmar it was reported that, 'Most of the farmhouses have been rebuilt, enlarged and improved ... and a considerable extent of the fields is inclosed [*sic*] with stone dikes ... Many acres of moory and marshy ground, that were useless and even offensive, are now producing remunerating crops of corn, grass, and trees of various kinds.'

The arrival of the railway from Aberdeen in 1859 had a dramatic effect on the life of several parishes. The planned extension of the Deeside line to Aboyne along the obvious route by the River Dee was abandoned due to a land dispute at Kincardine O'Neil. Instead the line went north from Banchory along a longer route with steep gradients through Glassel and Torphins to Lumphanan and back to the Dee at Dess. This route to Lumphanan followed an earlier plan, which had been abandoned, to build a line from Banchory to Alford via Cushnie.

Colonel Thomas Innes of Learney recognised the potential of the coming of the railway to Torphins and welcomed its construction over his land. In 1857 Torphins consisted of a few thatched cottages and an old inn but its development following the arrival of the railway was dramatic. The town continues to grow despite the predictions of A. Derek Farr, who in his book *Stories of Royal Deeside's Railway* (1971) stated, 'Apart from a small maternity home and a hotel, Torphins contains very little and is bound to decline again now that the rail line has gone.' He did not of course know what effect the discovery of North Sea oil would have on the economic development and potential for the villages of Midmar and Cromar. In the past 30 years crofts and castles have been renovated and rebuilt, businesses established and schools rejuvenated.

Midmar Castle is one of the remarkable group of north-east gems all built by the famous Aberdeenshire family of master masons, the Bels of Balogy (the old name for Midmar). It is known that George Bel was responsible for the building of the castle and he is buried in the neighbouring kirkyard. The inscription on his simple grave slab reads 'HEIR LYIS GEORG BEL MEASON DECEISIT IN BALOGY ANO 1575'. The lands of Midmar were owned by the Gordons, a branch of the Huntly family.

Midmar Castle from East.

The castle stands on the lower northern slopes of the Hill of Fare and was built on a Z-plan for Alexander Gordon, fourth Laird of Midmar, sometime after 1564. In 1594 this Laird took part in the rebellion of the Catholic lords and as a result the Earl Marischal, acting on the order of King James VI, burned and destroyed part of the castle. Between 1603 and 1609 the fifth Laird had the castle remodelled, but in 1640 it was sold to the Forbes of Tolquhon. Over the years the castle has had several owners and the late Queen Mother expressed some interest in the property prior to her purchase of Castle of Mey. In 1977 the empty castle was bought, re-harled and restored to some of its former glory.

The Cottage, Midmar, once a shop and now the Midmar Inn, is situated on the main Aberdeen—Tarland road some distance from the main settlement of Midmar and Comers. In its heyday the shop was not only the provider of groceries and other essential requirements of the locals, but it also displayed a notice 'Licensed to sell Porter and Ale'. As the nearest pub was some miles away in Echt, the shop provided what has been described as 'a close, if unlawful rival' when drink was consumed on the premises (which was actually illegal). There is also a story that the road to the west was haunted and few would venture along it alone at night, so a few drinks at the Cottage alehouse were required to gain the courage to walk on up the wooded stretch of the road into the open at Lurg.

Corsindae House dates from the sixteenth century. The original wing is on the right of the photograph and the entrance lay between the two turrets. The first owners were a branch of the Forbes family and one John Forbes was described by a government official as one of 'the insolent society of boyis denounced for slaughter and other enormities'. In 1605 he was arrested by Irvine of Drum and taken by strong guard to Edinburgh to be put on trial for his misdeeds.

Midmar old school was closed in 1880 and the original girls' school of Corsindae was enlarged to cater for the extra pupils (upper). Over the years the school saw many extensions and improvements and up to the 1960s was a junior secondary school providing education for pupils from the ages of five to fifteen. In 1955 the school had three full-time, one part-time and three visiting teachers and a roll of 74 pupils. In those days a few pupils moved on from Midmar at fifteen and were given transport to schools in Aberdeen. A new primary school was built in the 1960s on the same site as the former junior secondary school and part of the building still remains, including the headteacher's house.

The lower picture shows the opening of Midmar Hall in 1905. Miss Fyffe-Duff of Corsindae gave the land on which it was built. The cost of its construction was £249 18/- and it was recorded that there was a 'stiff annual feu duty of £8'.

Birley Brae, also known as Comers Brae, was the particularly steep road leading down into Comers. Here, two alternative forms of transport can be seen on the brae. The first mention of public transport in the parish appears in the early 1880s when Charles Fowler ran a horse bus from Birley to Aberdeen; later John Davie had a mail bus to connect with the Echt—Aberdeen service. This was followed by Goodalls and then Alexanders provided a regular service to and from Aberdeen. Today, the route is served by Stagecoach buses which run between Tarland and Aberdeen.

Comers

One of the reasons that this district attracted a settled population is given by the Rev. George Cook in the *New Statistical Account* of 1842. He described the topography thus: 'The surface of the parish is very uneven, being elevated into hill ridges, and, of course, depressed by their accompanying vales. Between the ridges flow rills or small burns from west to east. The ridges are of so gentle acclivity as to offer no obstacle to the plough from the bottom to the summit, and, if properly tilled, produce fair crops, both green and white, unless where the soil is so thin as not to admit of ploughing.' As a result farming became the main occupation of the area and it continued to be right up to the middle of the twentieth century when the drift away from the land brought massive depopulation. However, the old crofts and houses have recently come back into their own and many of these houses have been converted and modernised and Midmar and Comers are beginning to flourish again. In the foreground in the general view is House of Comers. The gable end of the adjoining house was the general store and post office which opened in 1877 (as seen on page 1).

Comers

In this photograph looking south over the farm of Gordon Laird, harvesting is in progress with all the family assisting. The crop had already been scythed and was being forked onto the cart. In the distance the 'stooks', a common sight in those days, are drying in the field. Comers shop is partly hidden right of centre and the steep Birley Brae can be seen further to the left. In 1881 David Angus was the first to venture down this steep and twisty brae with a traction engine and a full load of coal.

Easter Tulloch was farmed by the Ross family from the late nineteenth century until about 1945. Four of the brothers - Alan, Bill, Jim and Donald - are shown here hard at work. Their eldest brother, Fred, worked at Midmar Castle. Jim, on the cart, was a noted ploughman in the area.

This photograph was taken at Easter Tulloch and possibly shows James Ross, the father of the brothers featured on the previous page. The building behind the bull is known as a chaumer and was the sleeping place for the farm workers.

The Learney Estate has been in the ownership of the Innes family for 200 years. Learney, from the Gaelic for 'place on the hill slope', was originally part of the Durward barony of Onele and then passed though the Irvines of Drum and the Forbes of Craigievar to the Brebner family in 1747. A house was built in 1750 and the estate was then inherited by William Innes, who had married Jane Brebner in the early nineteenth century. The central block was destroyed by fire in 1837 and rebuilt, but the final chapter in the evolution of the house was the work of Colonel Thomas Innes, who redesigned the two wings in the late 1860s. Through his many contributions to the local community, Colonel Innes was regarded as the founder of modern Torphins and died, aged 98, in 1912. His descendants have given further distinction to the family by providing two Lord Lyon King of Arms in recent years.

Less than three miles south east of Torphins is Glassel. In *The Agricultural Survey of Kincardineshire* (1807) it is recorded that up to 1783, of the 690 acres of the estate, only about thirty acres of it were ploughable. The laird at the time was a Mr Baxter, a London banker, who set about improving the ground. Stones were removed and were used to fill drains, make roads, and also build walls around the fields. Some of these walls were up to twelve or sixteen feet thick and were known as 'consuming dykes'. The book also recorded that the price for the work was eight pounds per acre for the removal of the stones and a further six pounds per acre for liming. The remains of two old lime kilns can still be seen on the estate. The book also describes Glassel House as 'a handsome and commodious modern mansion, having pretty extensive and laid out gardens, with a hot-house and some beautiful shrubbery.' Although there has been extensive modernisation over the years, the house and estate could be described in very similar terms today.

In the general view of Glassel the shop is on the left and the station on the right. The station was opened in December 1859 when the Deeside railway was extended to Aboyne. Just why a station was built there is a mystery, but it must be remembered that although there were few houses in the immediate vicinity the railway served a wider community who were dependent on it for their transport. The station and the adjoining property, which was occupied by the stationmaster, are now private houses. The shop, opened in 1899, was a real necessity in those days. Not only did it provide the locals with all their general needs, but it also had a post office. The old shop at Glassel is now a private house called Tanglewood.

In the 1950s the laird of Easter Beltie built the hall, which was named after him, to provide facilities for the social events of the people of Campfield and Glassel. The hall, however, was made available for others to use and on the reverse of the card on which this photograph was printed is an advertisement: 'The Milne Hall has a Two Acre Field attached which is ideal for Picnics, Parties, Campers and Hikers. WRI Outings specially catered for. All communications to be sent to – The Shop, Glassel, Tel Number Torphins 34.

Craigmyle House used to stand on an elevated site about a mile north east of Torphins. The lands of Craigmyle belonged to a cadet branch of the Burnetts of Leys and the house was probably built around 1696 by Isabel Burnett of Craigmyle and her husband, John Farquharson of Invercauld. The house was extended and modernised in 1902 under the direction of the architect Sir Robert Lorimer. In 1960 it was demolished and later a modern bungalow was built on the site which retains the triple arch loggia and granite front door piece of the 1902 house. A short distance from the original house was a grand old tree known locally as the 'Darnley Ash', though it is extremely unlikely that Lord Darnley planted it. Indeed the tale that Lord Darnley visited Craigmyle after the Battle of Corrichie, fought nearby on the Hill of Fare in 1562, is certainly without foundation - he was in England at the time. The tree was cut down in 1960.

A view looking north along the Kincardine O'Neil road through Torphins. The Learney Hall can be seen in the distance on the left and on the right is the spire of the Free Church, built in 1905. In 1941 the congregation of this church entered into a union with the North Church, which had been erected in 1876 on Learney ground, and the latter became the parish church. The Free Church continued to be used as a church hall for some time, but has since been sold and is now used as a pine furniture workshop. The cottages on the right are of particular interest. Now called Laigh Riggs, these former alms houses were bought in the late 1950s by Sir Thomas Innes to convert into his own home when he left Learney House to his son Thomas. He added a small tower-like porch at the rear on which the Innes family arms can be seen.

PUTTING GREEN AND TENNIS COURTS, TORPHINS

214493

The original bowling green and tennis courts at Torphins date from 1885, but the years have seen many changes. This photograph was taken in 1931 – much still remains today, but the putting green has gone and has been replaced by new tennis courts. The bowling green has been upgraded and now has a new pavilion.

Torphins   19

G. TAYLOR'S JUVENILE DANCING CLASS, TORPHINS. 1909.

Alice Berry.

This 1909 photograph was taken outside the Learney Hall, which was built of grey granite in 1898 by Sir Francis Innes to celebrate the sixtieth wedding anniversary of his parents. The dance master, Mr G. Taylor, stands on the right – he was known locally as Dancing Doddie - and the provider of the music is on the left, clutching his violin.

This distinctive building, the Star and Griffin, on the road to Lumphanan was built in the early 1930s on land – reputedly used for rearing pigs – owned by Sir Thomas Innes of Learney. He gave permission for the building provided it incorporated the names of emblems on the Innes family arms. The original owners of the Sunshine Café, Miss Leask and Miss Black, moved from a shop on the Square where they sold sweets and ice cream. The café was a great attraction for locals and tourists and was even able to provide accommodation for small wedding receptions. It is now a children's nursery school and the Star and Griffin a private house.

Both the road and railway to Lumphanan can be seen in this view, with a passenger train travelling towards the viaduct and Satan's Den. The house in the foreground was the Home Farm and the large barn-like building in front of the train was the workshop of Robertson the joiner. The open fields have long since been developed for housing while the land on the right of the farmhouse would later be used for the building of the Sunshine Café and the Star and Griffin.

SATAN'S DEN, NEAR LUMPHANAN.

Leaving Torphins, the railway line passed through a cutting before moving out over a five-span viaduct high over the Beltie Burn. The line then continued into a steep rocky cutting at Tillychin known as Satan's Den. During the winter months deep snow drifts were liable to block the line at this point. Although the Deeside line was closed in 1966, it was not until 1989 that the viaduct was demolished. It had been expected that it would take a week to complete the job but when the first arch across the Tornaveen road was taken down the others fell like a set of dominoes. Within half an hour the viaduct had fallen and the famous landmark was no more.

The village of Lumphanan owes much to the building of the Deeside Railway which was opened from Banchory to Aboyne on 2 December 1859. The station was a busy place and in its day had a stationmaster, a signalman and a porter. The line closed for passenger traffic on 28 February 1966.

On the ground adjacent to the station, and served by the branch line which can be clearly seen in the foreground, were the agricultural sheds and mart establish in 1911, the lime company, and oil storage tanks. All of this added greatly to the use of the station for the forwarding of goods. Between 1864 and 1938 this decreased dramatically from 2,639 tons to 267 tons. Livestock was also carried but by 1938 this had ceased altogether and goods trains stopped using the station in June 1964.

The story of Macbeth as told by Shakespeare is far from the truth. Macbeth became king in 1040 and ruled for seventeen years and he was not the bloodthirsty tyrant as portrayed by the playwright. Macbeth's association with Lumphanan has many reminders of his last battle, but over time folklore has grown up regarding the various features. There is Macbeth's Stone, where Macduff overtook the king and where he was wounded, or perhaps even killed; Macbeth's Well, where he may have stopped to drink (although an alternative story suggests that his severed head was washed there before being carried in triumph to Malcolm Canmore); Macbeth's Cairn, on the southern slopes of Perkhill, where it is claimed he met his death in a hand-to-hand struggle with Macduff. The cairn, however, probably dates from prehistoric days and most certainly was not the burial spot for Macbeth – he is buried in Iona. The cairn was of considerable size until the nineteenth century when the farmer of Craigton removed many of the stones to build dykes. Afterwards, when further trenching of the hillside around the cairn was carried out, many of the gathered stones were deposited on the cairn. Thus many of the boulders that are there today may not be the original ones. It was at this time that steps were taken to protect the cairn and the encircling dyke was built and a ring of trees were planted between the outer dyke and the cairn. In 2005, to mark the millennium of Macbeth's birth, Lumphanan held a day of celebration and a special granite stone weighing about 200lbs and engraved '1005 – 2005' was carved at the Tarland granite works and the local blacksmith hand-made the metal ring on the top of it. The stone is now placed in the community garden opposite the Macbeth Arms Hotel.

HOTEL

MACBETH ARMS HOTEL

ALBERT F. LAW

MACBETH ARMS HOTEL, LUMPHANAN.

With the arrival of the railway in 1859, the old Kirkton of Lumphanan was not only left stranded half-a-mile west of the station but it was separated from the old St Finan's Kirk by the intervening railway line. Thus the development of a new village started at the expense of this once rural area. Soon afterwards the Lumphanan Hotel and the adjoining shop were built. By 1918 over 30 new houses had been added to the two small crofts and the toll bar which had existed before the arrival of the railway. The licensed grocer next door with the four distinctive arches was at one time owned by Albert F. Law and next door to that was the Town and County Bank. At one time there was also the North of Scotland bank in the village, but the two banks amalgamated in 1907 and became the North of Scotland and Town and County Bank and later the Clydesdale and North of Scotland Bank. Today, there is no bank at all in Lumphanan.

A view looking north up Perkhill Road, with the spire of Stothert Memorial Church standing at the top of the hill on the right of the road. Formerly the Free Church, it dates from 1870 and is named in memory of the Rev. Thomas Stothert who was chiefly responsible for its building. On the left, at the foot of the road, was the general merchant's shop of Robert Moir. His son, David, later sold the shop to the Scottish Co-operative Wholesale Society. On the opposite side of the road is an early lamp standard next to where the war memorial was erected after the Great War. There was opposition in the village when streetlighting was first proposed because of the extra expense, but when it was improved and linked with the North of Scotland Hydro-Electric Board it warranted favourable comment in the *Third Statistical Account* (1952). Behind the streetlight is the shop at one time owned by George Merchant, 'Furnishing Tailor'.

D'ye min on Geordie Ellis
At the smiddy, aside the dam
Ca'in at the bellas
Wi' a horse shoe in his hand?

The Mill Dam and, in the foreground, a wheel axle in the yard of the local smiddy. Alas, the smiddy is no more and in recent years housing has been built on much of this area. Reflected in the water are, on the left, the shop and house at the foot of Perkhill and on the right the Public Hall, built in 1897. Adjoining it is another shop, now a house, and the Home Farm with traditional haystacks clearly in view.

Just over a mile south west of Lumphanan is Auchenhove (sometime spelled as Auchinhove) and nearby the site of the Loch of Auchlossan. In 1859 the proprietors of the adjoining lands – the Marquis of Huntly and Farquharson of Finzean, who at that time was the landlord of Auchenhove - formed a scheme to drain it and so provide additional land for cultivation. James W. Barclay (later MP for Forfarshire) and his brother, who were well known in the area as seedsmen and agricultural suppliers, undertook the work. When the Barclays gave up their interest in the farm of Mains of Auchlossan the reclaimed land was divided between that farm and East Mains of Auchenhove. It was soon after that the loch started re-appearing and taking back control of a large acreage and it was not until the Second World War that the government stepped in to once again reclaim the land for agricultural use as part of the war effort. Today, the land has dried up again but for how long is hard to forecast. Also in the area are the ruins of the Castle of Auchenhove. The Duguids of Auchenhove held considerable power in the district from the middle of the fifteenth century, but as a result of siding with Bonnie Prince Charlie the laird watched from the Hill of Coull as his house was burnt to the ground by the troops of the Duke of Cumberland. About half a mile from the old castle was the Howff of Auchenhove which, it has been claimed, was used as the burial place of the Duguids of Auchenhove. The present Auchenhove House dates from the nineteenth century and was originally built as a dower house for the laird of Finzean. The lands of Auchenhove were sold in 1888 when they were purchased by Charles Stephen Leslie and since that time there have been several changes of ownership.

AUCHINHOVE

For many years the people in the community of Milton of Auchenhove were served by the general merchant's shop of A. Reid. It must be remembered that in the early days of the last century, with limited means of transport, Lumphanan was quite isolated and the local shop was of great importance. Like so many other small shops in the hinterland of the area, it closed in the 1960s and was converted into a private house now known as Sunnybrae Cottage.

Tornaveen, a small hamlet on the Aberdeen—Tarland road, was able to sustain its own shop and post office. Many people in the area will remember Peter Cruickshank who owned the shop until his death in the late 1970s. With no hope of the shop being taken over, the property was converted into a private house now known as Thistlebrae. The nearest shop to Tornaveen is now at Perkhill, some two miles to the west.

On Tuesday, 12 February 1929, the *Aberdeen Press and Journal* reported that 'Germany and Deeside were linked yesterday with dramatic suddenness in an episode of the air which gives cogent point to the well-worn axiom that truth is stranger than fiction'. On the previous Sunday three Germans had set out on a short balloon trip from near Leipzig only to be battered by gale-force winds which carried them out of control over France and the North Sea. The balloonists eventually crossed over Aberdeen and crash-landed near the farm of Claydykes at Tornaveen, over 1,000 miles and 19 hours after they had set off. The three men - Herr Paul Rohr, the commander, Dr Gerd Rexhausen, and Herr Paul Thiclecke, a dentist - escaped with only superficial injuries. They were looked after initially by local farmers, the Clarks of Claydykes and the Cargills of Newton of Tornaveen. Peter Cruickshank, the owner of the Tornaveen Post Office, then took them by car to Torphins where they were refreshed at the Learney Arms before being taken to Aberdeen.

About 1862 a meeting house without denominational restrictions was built in Tornaveen. Today, this building is still in use and services are still held from time to time. St Erchard, one of the many Celtic saints, provides an interesting link between Tornaveen and Kincardine O'Neil. Not only is Tornaveen in the parish of Kincardine O'Neil, but St Erchard was - according to tradition - born at Tolmauds near Tornaveen and Ennets, a place name in the immediate neighbourhood, is still preserved and denotes a sacred foundation. St Erchard is said to have entered the monastery of St Ternan at Banchory and died at Kincardine O'Neil where a well bearing his name can still be seen.

At one time a thriving school served the widespread community of Tornaveen. The much earlier school (top picture) was replaced by a well-built new school, although this too closed in the 1960s. In the late 1950s the school still had nineteen pupils but when it finally closed the numbers were down to six and they were transferred to Torphins Primary School. The school is now a private house.

Mill of Ennets was once a thriving and busy mill, but today this well-preserved building is a private house. At the turn of the last century there were five meal mills in the parish but not one remains as a working mill. The low level of agricultural wage compared with the wages on offer elsewhere sounded the death knell of so much of the farming industry. Farming was not the only industry which has seen a dramatic recession – whereas there were seven smiddies in the parish in 1900, only two remained in 1960 and there are none today. Granite quarrying, which once thrived at Hill of Fare and Sundayswells, has also now ceased. However, the quarry at Craiglash, near Torphins, remains and still provides bottoming for Aberdeenshire roads.

Craigievar Castle is one of Scotland's best preserved tower houses. William Forbes, known as Danzig Willie, made his fortune through trade with northern Germany and invested his wealth in the building of the castle between 1610 and 1626. The castle, the work of the Bel family responsible for the building of many of the castles in north-east Scotland, has externally remained virtually unaltered and very much resembles a fairytale castle. It is claimed that it was the inspiration for Walt Disney's Cinderella's Castle in Disneyland and which has become a feature of all the Disney Parks throughout the world. The castle remained in the ownership of Willie Forbes's descendants until 1965 when it passed into the ownership of the National Trust for Scotland.

In days gone by Milton of Cushnie, in the parish of Leochel-Cushnie, relied solely on agriculture. As can be seen from this photograph the cultivation once extended far up the hillsides and this was achieved by the hard work of horse and plough. It is recorded that before the Second World War there were not more than three tractors in the whole parish.

In 1871 the population of the parish of Leochel-Cushnie peaked at 1232 and from that date declined to a figure of 692 in 1951. With little work for the young, emigration - especially to Canada and Australia - was responsible for some of the decline. This has been partially reversed by a new population which has come to live in the area. Many of the older houses in Milton of Cushnie, some built of granite, have in recent years been converted into comfortable modern dwellings.

MILTON OF CUSHNIE.

The school at Cushnie was closed in the 1960s and the pupils transferred to Craigievar Primary. In 1951 there were 42 pupils at Cushnie and after the age of eleven they transferred to O'Neill Corse which at that time was a junior secondary; some moved onto one of the three senior secondary schools in the area - Banchory, Inverurie or Huntly. The *Third Statistical Account* of the 1950s noted that 'the value of education is increasingly appreciated by parents, but there is also a general feeling that with the new leaving age of fifteen, a boy destined for farming loses more in physical vigour than he gains in mental alertness in the extra year.' At the turn of the twentieth century every farm had its mill. At threshing time the bulk of the work was usually done by hiring in a steam mill, which was very labour intensive. The farmer would borrow workers from neighbouring farms and in return lend some of his when required. By the 1950s, because of a drastic reduction in the work force, this system was becoming increasingly difficult to maintain.

A hundred years ago most villages in the area had their outdoor curling pond and when the weather was cold enough and the water frozen a bonspiel would be held. Cushnie's curling pond was situated near Cushnie Lodge and was opened sometime before 1904. The curling pond was popular up to the late 1930s but then fell into disuse. The scene is typical of the day – the men all wearing their 'bunnets' on their heads and well dressed for the occasion. The centre of the 'house', the target for the stones, is marked by what is known as the 'bottle' (clearly seen in the picture). The brooms used by the players to brush the ice are somewhat different from those used today and are very much the typical witch's broom. Some claim that curling originated in Scotland and the name is derived from the ability to make the stone curl by 'birling' (turning) the handle of the stone as the player releases it. Because of the distinctive sound the stone makes as it travels along the ice, curling is often referred to as 'the roaring game'.

The Cromar Valley, with the Grampians in the background, offers one of Scotland's finest views and is often referred to as the Queen's View. There is now a hill indicator plaque at the viewpoint at the Slack of Tillylodge in the foreground where the road from Aberdeen enters the Howe of Cromar. The plaque was erected by the Deeside Field Club in 1970 to mark its jubilee and on it is a verse from a poem by George Stephen which captures the scene: *'Lo, what a prospect meets the eyes/ When gazing raptured o'er Cromar,/ Beyond the Grampian peaks arise/ The crowning heights of Lochnagar'*. A planning proposal to quarry over three million tonnes of granite and crush it to make aggregate on an eight-hectare site on the steep slopes of Craiglich was thankfully rejected in April 2005. The objectors to the proposal not only argued that it would have a detrimental affect on the Queen's View, but that it would destroy valuable habitats of protected species such as the badger and the red squirrel.

CROMAR VALLEY, SHOWING THE GRAMPIAN'S

Alexander MacRobert bought the small house and farm of Burnside in 1888 as a home for his ageing parents. The farm was renamed Douneside and when his parents died in the early 1900s he decided to turn Douneside into a small country mansion and added a tower and, later, two wings. Alexander was manager of Cawnpore Woollen Mills and was knighted in 1911 for his services to industry in India. His first wife had died while he was over there and Rachel, whom he married in 1911, developed the splendid gardens which are still a feature of the house today. They had three sons, Alasdair, Roderic and Iain, who all spent a happy childhood at Douneside. Their father died in 1922, the same year in which he was created first Baronet of Cawnpore and Cromar. Tragedy was to hit the family in 1938 when the first son, Alasdair, was killed in a flying accident. When war broke out in 1939 the two remaining sons joined the Royal Air Force. Roderic was killed in May 1941 and the following month Iain was lost on a flying operation. Lady MacRobert donated £25,000 to the nation to purchase a Stirling bomber, which she asked to be named 'MacRobert's Reply'. Two years later she set up the MacRobert Trust, which to this day continues to award grants. Lady MacRobert is also remembered for her interest in farming and pedigree cattle, and this continued right up to her death in 1954. Douneside then became the headquarters of the MacRobert Trust and remained so until 1970 when it was moved to Balmuir on the outskirts of Tarland. Thereafter, Douneside was converted to a leave centre for the three services and in recent years has been increasingly used as a conference centre.

Shortly after their marriage, the seventh Earl of Aberdeen and his wife, Ishbel, paid a visit from Haddo to the family's Cromar estate. She fell in love with the Tarland countryside and persuaded the Earl to build a house, completed in 1905, which they called House of Cromar. The Earl became a Marquis in 1916 and in 1919 he reached an agreement with Sir Alexander MacRobert under the terms of which the house and estate of Cromar would pass to Sir Alexander, or his heirs, on the death of the Marquis. He died in 1934 but Lady MacRobert continued to live in Douneside and only used House of Cromar for special occasions. In 1943 she endowed the House of Cromar, renamed Alastrean House, as a rest centre for operational crew of the Royal Air Force and Commonwealth Air Force. It continued to be used as such after the war, but in 1951 Alastrean House was damaged by fire. It was rebuilt and reopened again in 1955. In 1984 it was leased to the Royal Air Force Benevolent Fund and converted to provide a permanent residential home. In May 1985 the first residents arrived, but by 2003 it looked as if the house would have to close because it was becoming too costly to run. But it received a reprieve and in March 2005 it became part of the Balhousie Care Group, although it is still owned by the MacRobert Trust.

In 1837 a branch of the Aberdeen Banking Company (later the Union Bank) was opened at the Lodge, Tarland, which at that time was called Indego (shown on some old maps as Indiego). The agent of the bank was Lord Aberdeen's factor. During the Great War the building was used as a convalescent home for wounded soldiers, being loaned by Lord and Lady Aberdeen for use as an auxiliary hospital under the supervision of the Red Cross Committee. It was opened for the reception of its first patients on 31 March 1915 and the local doctor acted as Medical Officer. Lord and Lady Aberdeen allowed the use of the grounds of House of Cromar by the patients and this included the tennis courts and golf course. When soldiers wished to attend the various church services held in Tarland, Lord Aberdeen also sent his motor car to take them to their place of worship.

Ishbel, Lady Aberdeen, was a frequent visitor to the home of Miss Margaret Anderson. Lady Aberdeen wrote of her: 'Miss Anderson's museum at the Roadside Cottage, Culsh, and the genuine old Pict's house hard by, are goals for many a pilgrimage. Would that all pilgrims were as well rewarded for their journeying as this who visit Margaret Anderson and listen to her stories of other days, illuminated as they are by pithy reflections and flashes of quaint humour, which send you home 'wi' gey muckle to think o''. An excellent account of the life and times of Margaret Anderson was written by the Marchioness of Aberdeen and Temair for the fourth edition of the *Deeside Field*, published in 1929. Margaret died in 1909 and her museum was left in the care of Lady Aberdeen who re-established it in Tarland. At the outbreak of the Great War the room in which it was kept was wanted for another purpose and the various items were sold or given back to the donors. Margaret is buried in the old churchyard at Migvie.

A view of Tarland from the bridge on the approach from the south. On the right is the garage which has now been replaced by housing. Next to it is the Town and County Bank, later the Clydesdale Bank and which is now closed. Next to the bank is the wooden faced building gifted to the people of Tarland by Lady Aberdeen and used by the Red Cross during the Great War. On the other side of the road, beyond the row of cottages, is the garage of Harry Nicoll who ran a bus service to Aboyne and Aberdeen. It is now the yard of the Tarland Granite Works. In the centre of the photograph is the familiar outline of the Aberdeen Arms Hotel.

On the extreme left of this view of Tarland's Square is George Grant's bakery – the photograph was taken after it was rebuilt following a fire which destroyed the premises sometime before 1914. The shop is now the pharmacy but the old bakery ovens can still be seen inside. The tower in the background belongs to Cromar Hall, built in 1889. The hall was replaced by a new building on the same site; the foundation stone of this was laid by Lady MacRobert in 1951 and it was opened four years later on 22 April 1955, amid controversy about who should manage it. By that time Lady MacRobert had died and a large section of the people of Tarland felt they were to have no say in the running of the new hall which was, they claimed, contrary to her wishes. The cost of the building, which was in excess of £30,000, was met from the MacRobert Trust. The MacRobert Memorial Hall was so named in commemoration of her three sons.

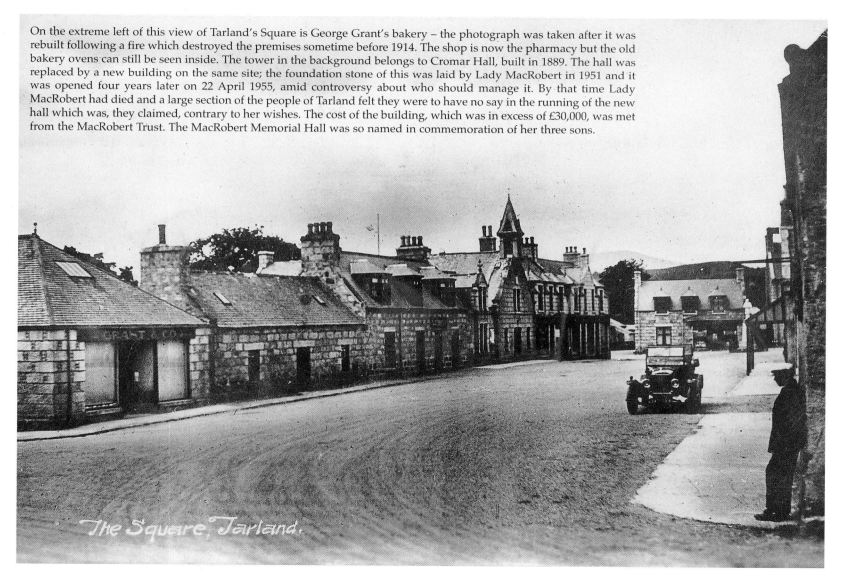

The Square, Tarland.

Further up Tarland's Square is Mowatt's shop, with the extended frontage, and at the west end two houses with shops below – on the left was the chemist's shop and on the right a watchmaker's shop. Note that the war memorial is missing which helps to date the picture to the early part of the last century.

On the right is the Aberdeen Arms Hotel in the Square, Tarland. The name is still the same today and is of course a reference to Lord Aberdeen, who at the time of its building was the local landowner. Many of the hotels on Deeside are named after the local laird, for example Irvine Arms, Drumoak; Burnett Arms, Banchor;, Gordon Arms, Kincardine O'Neil; Huntly Arms, Aboyne; and Fife Arms, Braemar.

Alexander Morren owned the general merchant's business on the left of this photograph of Tarland's Square and he published the *Cromar War Memorial Book* as a tribute to the many men and women from the area who served in the Great War. On the war memorial are inscribed the names of those from Cromar - comprising the villages of Coull, Logie Coldstone (Logie-Coldstone is the parish as opposed to the village), Migvie and Tarland - who lost their lives fighting for their country. In the far distance are the ruins of the old parish church and churchyard, now preserved as an ancient monument. The walls and the belfry still remain but the bell is now missing. On the grassy ground in front of the churchyard is the memorial to Peter Milne, the 'Tarland Minstrel' who was a famous violinist and composer of Scottish music. Milne's later life was dogged by misfortune and he died a pauper in 1908 in Aberdeen. The monument was erected in 1932, largely due to the efforts of Alex Innes who had the shoemaker's shop adjoining the present post office. On the memorial are these words from a poem by Robert Burns: '*Riches denied, thy boon was purer joys,* / *What wealth could never give nor take away*'. In front of the churchyard can be seen a fountain erected in 1913 in memory of Francis Donaldson, a farmer at the Boig.

The thatched cottages on Melgum Road were in the oldest part of Tarland, on the road leading to what was once the Market stance where at one time regular markets and fairs were held throughout the year. Prior to 1799 four landlords held the whole village in lease from the Earl of Aberdeen. The tenants were subject to changes imposed on them at will by their landlords and as the *New Statistical Account* of 1842 reports: 'This arrangement was found hostile to industrious improvement and ordinary comfort, and to promote indifference, idleness, dissipation and immorality'. New leases were granted in 1799 and Lord Aberdeen gave every householder in the village their own piece of ground. The villagers were thus encouraged to build comfortable houses and to work their small piece of ground. The *New Statistical Account* continued: 'Such laudable exertion in a few years evinced its happy efforts, when each villager might be possessed of his cow and horse, and the family supplied with meal and malt, butter and cheese, and vegetables equal to their consumpt'. These old houses have all now either disappeared or have been much altered. The house on the left, which dates from the early 1900s, still remains, but the old water hydrant on the edge of the footpath has gone.

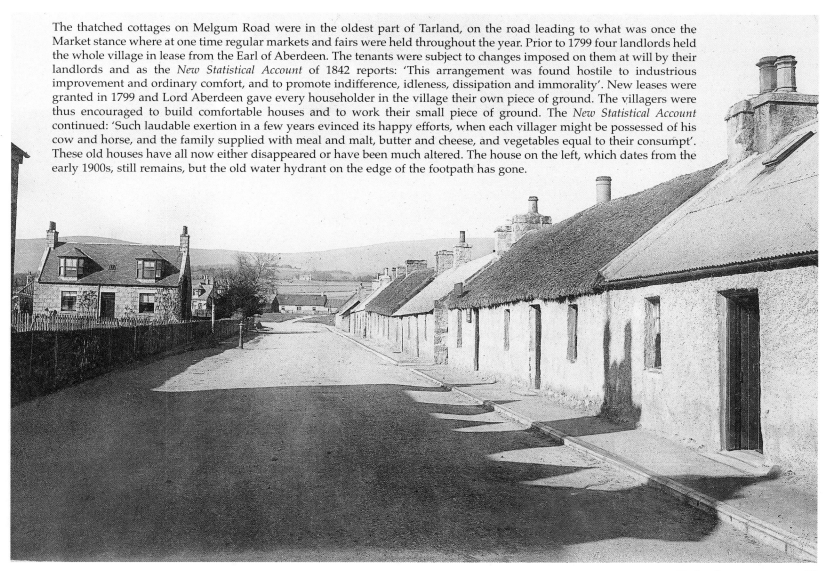

The *Third Statistical Account* of the Parish of Logie-Coldstone, written in 1950, describes the area as one of 'great natural beauty, and looking southwards from the high ground on the north, affords a wonderful panoramic view over a wide expanse of Deeside'. Logie-Coldstone is in two parts – Logie, the flat southern half, and the hilly area of Coldstone to the north. The name of the village of Newkirk dates from 1618 when the two parishes were united and a kirk was built there which was more central for both districts. This parish church was rebuilt in 1780 and over the years this solid and impressive building has undergone many alterations, a later addition being the steeple. In 1984, as a result of church amalgamations, it closed and is now a private house, complete with a swimming pool in what was once the nave. In 2005 the original bell from the church tower was gifted to a church in Kasseh, Ghana. The congregation there were delighted to receive the bell, which bears a Latin inscription – *Michael Burgerhuis me fecit* ('Michael Burgerhuis made me') - and the date 1619. It was cast that year in the Netherlands.

There are numerous springs in the parish of Logie-Coldstone, but the one that attracted the most attention during the nineteenth century was the strong chalybeate mineral spring a little to the south of the parish church. It was given the name Poldhu (Poll-dubh) which in Gaelic means 'the dark pool' - so called from the colour of the water as it flowed into a mossy hollow a few yards from its source. It has been claimed that water from the spring was used successfully to treat what, in earlier times, were called 'gravellish and scorbutic disorders', a disease resembling scurvy. When the healing powers of the Pannanich Wells, near Ballater, were discovered fewer people used the waters, but those that did still claimed it was a cure for all manner of disorders.

Logie Coldstone Curling Club House

Curling has been played on Deeside for over 120 years and in Scotland as a whole for much longer. In the 1780s Robert Burns wrote of the game - 'The sun had clos'd the winter day, / The curlers quat their roaring play'. Outdoor curling is a game dependent on weather and Logie Coldstone can claim to have been the coldest place in Britain in 1927, 1933, 1948, 1952 and 1958. On 14 March 1958 a temperature of -22.8°C was recorded – the lowest temperature recorded in the twentieth century at Logie Coldstone. The curling pond dates from the late 1800s. Notice the crampet leaning against the bank - this was an iron foot board used by the curlers to stand on when delivering their stones. On the verandah of the Curling Club House which still stands are some curling stones and brushes.

Newkirk grew up around the church and in 1951 the writer of the *Third Statistical Account* noted that the village comprised 24 houses and that in addition there was a school, church, post office and merchant's shop. Since that date the village has lost its church, post office and shop, but a new school which took the place of the one that burnt down in 1968 remains and serves the whole parish of Logie Coldstone. In recent years, Newkirk has seen many new houses being built. The view here is looking up Sunnybrae which runs from the former church to Sandy Heugh, an area of fine white sand. The building on the far left was once the stable where Willie Archibald kept his horses which he used for the pony and trap service he ran before World War I. On the far right the larger of the two gable ends was the old schoolhouse and to the right of it an old thatched cottage, long since gone. The writer of the *Third Statistical Account* mentions that by 1950 a thatched house or 'cot stob-thackit, wi twa timmer-lums' was becoming a thing of the past.

Tillypronie House, situated to the north of Logie Coldstone, was built by Sir John Clark, son of Sir James Clark who was physician to Queen Victoria. It was Sir James who had recommended the climate of the Dee Valley to the Queen and after several visits to the old Balmoral Castle she bought the estate in 1852 and started on the building of the new castle. Sir James, who had settled at Birkhall in 1848, sold the property to the Queen and purchased Pronie estate in 1855. At first the family stayed in the old farmhouse of Pronie until the new Tillypronie House was built in 1867. Tillypronie was frequently visited by the Queen, who was usually accompanied by her faithful servant, John Brown. It is said that he considered himself too grand to dine with the Clark's domestic staff and a special hut was built outside the front door of the house to which his meals were taken for him to eat in solitude. The American author Henry James, on a visit in 1878, wrote that 'this supremely comfortable house – lying deep among the brown and purple moors - enjoys a glorious view of sweeping hills and gleaming lochs that are forever before the windows'. Lord and Lady Royden purchased the house in 1925 and made many improvements to it and the gardens. In 1951 Gavin Astor purchased the estate and the present owner is his son, the Hon. Philip Astor, who allows the house to be rented for corporate events and special occasions. During the Second World War the house was let to Albyn School in Aberdeen and the boarders of the kindergarten and lower school moved there for safety. The senior school boarders and some of the day pupils were housed at nearby Blelack House.